Amazing Americans

George Washington

Sharon Coan, M.S.Ed.

Meet George Washington.

He was a farmer.

He got married.

He wanted America to be free.

He led the **army**.

He was **brave**.

He worked hard.

George was the first **president**.

GEORGE WASHINGTON

Ask It!

George Washington was an amazing American. Ask an adult to help you find an amazing American.

Tyler and Elbert

Tyler thinks Elbert is an amazing American. Elbert is Tyler's dad. Elbert is a doctor. He helps people feel better.

Ask how he or she helps people.

Glossary

army—a group who fights for a country

brave—not afraid

president—leader of a country

Index

Your Turn!

George had a busy life. Draw some of the things he did. Tell about your drawing.

Consultants

Diana Cordray
Education Center Manager
George Washington's
Mount Vernon

Shelley Scudder
Gifted Teacher
Broward County Schools

Caryn Williams, M.S.Ed.
Madison County Schools
Huntsville, AL

Publishing Credits

Conni Medina, M.A.Ed., *Managing Editor*
Lee Aucoin, *Creative Director*
Torrey Maloof, *Editor*
Lexa Hoang, *Designer*
Stephanie Reid, *Photo Editor*
Rachelle Cracchiolo, M.S.Ed., *Publisher*

Image Credits: Cover, p.1 Wikimedia Commons; pp.2, 9 Everett Collection Inc/Alamy; p.13 Ivy Close Images/Alamy; p.5 Pictorial Press Ltd/Alamy; p.11 Stocktrek Images, Inc./Alamy; pp.3, 6–7, 14, 17 The Granger Collection, New York/The Granger Collection; p.18 LOC [LC-DIG-pga-01368]/ The Library of Congress; p.8 LOC [LC-USZC2-3154]/ The Library of Congress; p.10 LOC [LC-USZC4-2737]/ The Library of Congress; p.22 KPA/United Archives/WHA/Newscom; Backcover Picture History/Newscom; pp.4, 12, 15–16 North Wind Picture Archives; All other images from Shutterstock.

Teacher Created Materials
5301 Oceanus Drive
Huntington Beach, CA 92649-1030
http://www.tcmpub.com

ISBN 978-1-4333-7352-7